Using Water to Make Electricity

Look at the water.

3

Here comes the water.

Splash!

Look at the **wheel.**

The water will go on the wheel.
The wheel will go round
and round and round.

9

The water will make electricity.

The electricity will make my **toothbrush** go.

13

The electricity will make my game go.

Glossary

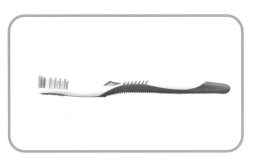 toothbrush

 wheel